When God Is Their Father *Too*:

"A Guide for Single-Parent Households"

Stephanie McCaskill

When God Is Their Father *Too*:
"A Guide for Single-Parent Households"

Copyright © 2020 by
Stephanie McCaskill
All rights reserved. No part of this book may be reproduced or transmitted in any form or by any means without written permission from the author.

ISBN (978-1-64713-710-6)

Disclaimer: Various versions of the bible were utilized in the production of this text. They are listed here as a reference but this list is not definitive: KJV, NKJV, NIV, MSG, NAS, & NLT

Acknowledgements

First, I must dedicate this book to Jesus Christ as my first fruit offering. Lord, I pray that I've made your heart smile.

To my husband, thank you for all of your moral and financial support. Sometimes, I stare at you in awe because God allowed you to be *"my Joseph."* The children and I, love and respect you greatly!

To my children, you all are the epitomized purpose *of* this book. All of the laughter, tears, and disagreements were used to bring God's purpose *for u*s to pass. I apologize for times you felt I didn't understand you; or seemed distant and unsupportive. Life, as a single parent... wasn't easy! However, I have never regretted being your mother. I love you all dearly.

To my grandbabies, I pray that I leave a legacy you won't find *too difficult* to follow. I pray that you *will* pass it along to *your* children. Granny, loves you so much.

To my siblings, Lisa, Alfred, Brian, Desiree, and Alexa I love you all with my *entire* heart. I appreciate your love and support.

To my Naomi, my Pastor, Apostle Dr. Cora B. Fells, thank you for allowing the Lord to use you as a vehicle for my deliverance. You sacrificed time, effort and finances to make my Christian Life one that I am proud of. Thank you, for never giving up on me. I love you so much!

To my Grace and Truth Family, what can I say about you all! Some of the older Saints are gone, but I wouldn't trade any of you for the world. Many times, you've rescued me and my children... and for that I am eternally grateful! I love you all.

To my daddy, thank you for always being in my life. Not a day goes by that I am not grateful for your love. You always had a way of making me feel special. Daddy, I love you!

To my grandma, the matriarch of our family, my chocolate drop, you are my backbone! Leaving Jacksonville was a big sacrifice, because I *did not* want to leave you. But through it all, you've always been by my side. Granny I pray I've made you proud. I love you dearly.

Table of Contents

Acknowledgements: iii

Introduction: vi

Chapters

1:    Mama, Daddy's Gone..1

2:    Mama, Make the Pain Go Away............................12

3:    Mama, Who Is *That* Man......................................21

4:    Mama, *Are* You Strong *Enough*...............................27

5:    Mama, *Can* You Jump Hurdles................................33

6:    Mama, You Need a *Man*..37

7:    Mama, We *Don't* Have Cable...................................46

8:    Mama, Remember ME..52

9:    Mama, *Aren't* You *Proud* of Me................................60

10:   Mama, I Remember *When*......................................63

11:   Mama, *Why* Am I Here...68

About the Author..79

Introduction

Greetings in the name of our Lord Jesus Christ. I am so blessed to have been chosen by God to accomplish *this* task He set before me. It is a privilege and an honor to encourage those who have found themselves in the position of being a single parent.

Please understand, I am not an expert on parenting. I am simply sharing my experiences to encourage others! This parenting journey is purposeful, and when purpose is coupled *with* destiny, sometimes we end up *alone*. "Alone," can be a scary place... but our alone time, with Jesus, will make us stronger! However, we do not reach this place of divine strength over night! The journey *is* unpredictable... thankfully, fastened seatbelts are provided and required for *this* ride!

Enjoy,

Stephanie

Chapter 1:
Mama, Daddy's Gone... The Reality

Key Scripture: Psalms 68:5 (KJV)

In a "perfect world," a family is made up of a father, mother and the children; perhaps maybe a pet: a goldfish, cat or dog. In this "perfect world," we sometimes feel like the people we love and those who profess to love us, will love and be with us forever. Surely, they would never walk out, and leave and plan to never come back...

We are all human that possess very real feelings and because of this, we are inclined to believe the best about people and hope that things will always be the way we desire. However, sometimes our "perfect world" *only* exits in our minds.

The harsh reality *is*... people do leave, die, and sometimes they never planned be a part of our "picture perfect" fantasy *anyway*. The Bible states in Matthew 24:12, Because of the iniquity that abounds, the love of many would wax cold." Oftentimes, when sin occurs in a person's life, it causes their love for others to diminish. If the *absent* parent has chosen to remain invisible... As the *present* parent, we must lovingly ensure "our children" that *it is not their* fault!

The "I" factor plays a powerful role in the life of someone who chose to walk out of his/her child's life. Some people have lost their parents because of an illness or untimely death... and they feel like their parental relationship *ended too soon*!

Single parents, it doesn't matter how the reality of single parenting manifested. What does matter is the realization that you're not in it *alone*. Without allowing pride to set in, [single parents] we must accept the help that is offered to us!

Trust me... (I know) it's easy to feel like we must handle everything on our own, but it is vital to accept help... Especially, the help of "God our Father!" Why, should we embrace God's helping hand... John 3:16 reveals the reality which is, "For God so loved the world, that He gave His only begotten Son, that whosoever believes in Him would not perish, but have everlasting life." Reality is that He's waiting to fill every void that is in our heart and we *are not alone!*

Psalms 68:5, states... God is the father to the fatherless and He places the lonely in a family. Genesis 22:14 declares, Jehovah Jireh our Father, will always supply us with what we need to make it in life. In your moment of weakness, God will be your strength. He will never leave you or forsake you. He will be with you unto the end of the world.

On the other hand, if you (the reader) are the absent parent, God has a healing for you too. Allow God to deliver you from that spirit of guilt, shame and defeat. You are stronger than you *think* you are. When we submit ourselves to the Lord Jesus Christ, He changes our lives. God is the mender of broken relationships, and it *is not* too late to start over.

I must take a pause here, and confess one of my many faults that Jesus delivered me from. I had a bad habit of not fully following various recipes when I cook. Measuring, what's that? Room temperature eggs, for what? I don't need to measure, and I can put cold eggs in my batter.

Well, after destroying countless dishes and baked goods, the Lord, ever so sweetly spoke to my heart and said, "Stephanie, you're not following the recipe..." The recipe provides the what, when, where, why, and how! Sometimes we become slightly over zealous about our lives and we start to add our own who, what, when, where, why, and how... Then we totally mess up God's "perfect will" (recipe) for our lives.

God has a plan and if we can *just* trust Him to know *that* He *knows* what He's doing... then everything will work out in our favor. He is the Master of Everything!

There is a young lady whom I know by the name of Emily whose parents were not married. Later in Emily's life, her father took a wife and they had children together. Emily felt rejected, broken, and abandoned. No matter what, her father and step mother desired to include her in their extended family structure. Often, she withdrew herself because she felt like, "The messed-up pancake" (this is the phrase she coined for her step family).

Emily tried to love and care for her siblings; however, she always questioned why her parents couldn't get married. She wanted to share her life with her biological mother and father... in *"their home,"* as a family unit. Emily perceived her siblings as perfect pancakes. Emily's logic was that her dad practiced with her... "the first pancake he ever made" and simply made a mess of things! However, he got it right on the second and third try.

This was an awfully deceptive plan that the enemy derived to cause hatred and bitterness in this young woman's heart. The enemy has caused her to suffer with depression, mental illness, suicidal thoughts, and murder. The feelings Emily felt were false, because the enemy blinded her from seeing the truth.

We must realize when we don't follow God's plan (the recipe), for our lives, we cause our seed to suffer. I explained to Emily that her parents conceived her out of wedlock... and when children are conceived outside of God's initial blueprint for the family unit, quite often children suffer emotionally, physically, mentally, and spiritually... that in turn brews hatred, envy, jealousy, strife, and malice towards the *absent* parent and others!

There is a young man named Ishmael. He was the product of an extramarital relationship. Ishmael's father was a married man and his mother was a single woman. Clearly, this was not God's plan, but it happened. It was not Ishmael's fault at all, and yet he suffered.

Ishmael's father and his father's wife agreed to provide shelter, food, and stability for the young man. One day, things changed, and his father and his father's wife felt it was time to break ties with Ishmael and his mother... because "the situation" caused a great deal of tension within their marriage.

Selfishly, they did not want their biological child to be affected by it (what about Ishmael?). The father really didn't want to break ties with Ishmael and his mother, but the Lord spoke to him and comforted his heart. The Lord told Ishmael's father, "I will bless Ishmael because he is *your* seed.

When Ishmael and his mother were exiled from the camp, they suffered greatly. His mother often cried and prayed, prayed and cried, wondering how she would take care of him. One day, she prayed because she could not provide food for Ishmael. He was hungry and thirsty, *but God...* provided nourishment for them.

The Lord consoled her heart and then He told her not to fear because He heard her cries and saw their needs. The Lord provided a well full of water for her and her son. They moved to a place that God guided them to and God became Ishmael's father as he grew and learned how to be a skillful survivor.

Originally, Ishmael's mother came from a different place, she was reared differently as a child. Her family practiced religious rituals and served idol gods, and they never believed in the one, true living God.

Since, Ishmael and his mother no longer attended church with his father, their faith was weakened and they stopped trusting in God.

As time went by, the Lord kept His promise to Ishmael's mother, and blessed Ishmael greatly. When he became of age, he took a wife and bore children. Those children had children, and those children had children. Ishmael became a mighty nation.

Even though God kept His promise to bless and meet the needs of Ishmael, He grew up with hatred in his heart towards his siblings. Today, Ishmael's children are very prosperous; however, because he felt abandoned, neglected, and betrayed... Ishmael developed a hateful heart, and he raised his children to feel the same way.

Ishmael's story is in the book of Genesis, chapters 16 through 21. The circumstances surrounding

Ishmael's life, occurred because his father did not follow the recipe that God had for his life. Ishmael's father allowed his self-pleasing, adulterous actions to plant seeds of unfruitful behaviors (the irony). If you're reading this and you have a similar story to Ishmael... Know and understand, "When your mother or father forsake you, the Lord will lift you up!"

To my brothers and sisters who are incarcerated, and your children are being raised by someone else, don't give up. You can have liberty in your soul right where you are. Forgive yourself and anyone else who may have wronged you or treated you unfairly. Seek to be a parent to your children. Pursue a loving relationship with them and the Lord can and will mend your parental relationship.

If you repent from your heart, God is faithful and just to forgive you of all your sins. He will cause your children to forgive you for anything and everything you've done. He is a restorer of relationships and a redeemer of time. The time you lost while you were *absent*, can and will be restored by God...

Give Him a chance and watch God move in your life. Jesus loves you, He died so you could overcome this emotional turmoil that has plagued you from the hands of the enemy. Even if you grew up in poverty and didn't have much, I want you to know the Lord was there the entire time watching over you... just as He did for Ishmael.

If you are the *domesticated/present* parent, do NOT instill hatred for the *absent* parent in your child. These actions will cause your child to suffer *even* more... when hatred, jealousy, and strife are present it torments the soul!

Teach your children to be forgivers, relationships can be healed, families can be restored. In essence, when we do this... as "their parents we teach our children not to make the same mistakes we made. God has a recipe for our lives. We must follow *the recipe* so we won't end up with "messed up pancakes!"

Let's make this even more clear, using Ishmael and his great nation as an example.

Please understand, although you may feel abandoned, angry, and full of hatred, I want you to know that your Heavenly Father God, Jesus Christ, was with you then and He still desires a relationship with you *now* because He loves you! Accept God's love today, He is a "life-changer!"

Intercession:

Father, in the name of Jesus, I pray for all single parents in the world who find it difficult to move pass the issue of being alone. Help my brother and my sister to accept you as their SOUL mate. I speak financial blessings and favor into their lives. Send supernatural help from the four corners of the globe to strengthen their hearts.

Most of all dear Lord, bring them to a place *in* you, that consumes their fears, abolishes low self-esteem, and love becomes and remains the foundation upon which they stand.

Jesus, I pray for the absent parents who are bound by Satan's hold. I speak freedom into their lives... right now in Your name. I command the enemy to release his grip NOW, so they can stand up and take their rightful place in YOUR kingdom and in the lives of their children... in Jesus' mighty name I pray. Amen!

Chapter 2:
Mama, Make the Pain Go Away...
The Healing

Key Scripture: Revelations 21:1-5 (KJV)

In my spare time, I enjoy watching those TV shows where they take an old, beat up, raggedy and forgotten about home and make it look brand new. I am quite sure if homes could talk, they would tell everyone how excited the families were when they purchased it.

If the walls could talk, they would tell stories about how the children were raised and reminisce about the fond memories that were made... Then at some point in the story, the tone would transition from happiness to unforgettable sadness... whether the transition occurred suddenly or intermittently – it wouldn't matter!

All that was left was a shell of what used to be or could have been. Now what used to be *a beautiful happy home* was now an *abandoned house in need of renovation* or possibly demolition. The dirt and mildew that now appeared to paint the exterior of the home was an indication of the dark sadness that had dwelled within the home.

Imagine a man casually strolled passed this dilapidated and abandoned house that *used* to be a home. When he saw it, he didn't pass judgment and ask it "How did you get like this?" But he looked at it through the eyes of mercy and saw what it could be again. He began to write down plans of how He could restore the home's glory with complete renovation.

Yes, it's true you were left and abandoned, possibly because of a selfish choice or by unforeseen circumstances; however, there is someone who's interested in you. He wants to take up habitation within you... in the midst of your pain.

I Peter 1:18-20, tells us how we were purchased a long time ago by the precious blood of Jesus Christ. It is time for the "for sale" sign to come down. For sale equates to emptiness and no longer desired by the original purchaser. God will always desire to reside within us and with us! God is ready to make the rough places smooth, uproot the hate and bitterness, and deliver anyone who lets Him in! The aforementioned things cause our temples to decay. Thankfully, Revelations 21:1-5 reassures us that Jesus will wipe away every tear we've cried... and quench our thirst forever!

If you're hurting today, and you have not allowed the Lord Jesus Christ to come in and heal you, now is the acceptable time. Start with forgiveness of the absent parent and also forgive yourself.

Yes, he or possibly she left, and yes people do die and transition to eternity; but if healing is to take place, we must allow ourselves to be whole and renewed. We must forgive the individuals that have hurt us and also ask for God's forgiveness, with a pure and sincere heart; so, that God's will be done in your life and in the life of the absent parent.

Let Him know that you're ready to become that "New Jerusalem," a Holy City *just* for Him! You will see God's glory manifest in your life. Your latter shall be greater than your former and then you shall be a "Temple fit for a King".

What is a Product? A person whose character and identity have been formed by a particular period or situation. It is imperative that the single parent who's raising the child allow himself to be healed. Because hurt people, hurt people. The last thing you should want is for the venom of past hurts to be spewed out upon your child.

Have you ever been in the presence of a mother or a father discussing the *absent* parent in a bad way? Those unseasoned words get into that child's heart and over time the hurt from them will transform into a desensitized person. They will begin to feel this is how it's supposed to be, so I've got to put up a guard and not allow anyone to hurt me like this. It will cause them to have issues in their own relationships. They feel like they can't trust anybody and it can cause them to continue this cycle perhaps in their own children.

As parents we should want what's best for our children. I don't know about anyone else, but I've never wanted my children to have looming "issues" from their upbringing. I always tried to identify any unclean spirits or unfavorable behaviors that tried to attack them… I prayed for protection and deliverance so those things did not spill over into their adulthood.

My oldest son was five when his father was killed. It was a very devastating experience because he loved his father. After a couple of months went by, Andre' began to complain of headaches when he woke up.

One day he wept profusely, and I asked, "Baby what's wrong?" He said, "I had a dream that I was at a park on a swing, and the devil started pushing the swing and I fell off and I hit my head..." and he always woke up with a headache.

I took Andre' to see Dr. Charles Simmons, a saved man (shout out), thankfully... the spiritual giftings of God reigned in his life. Dr. Simmons asked "Have any traumatic events recently occurred in Andre's life?"

Surprised at what he asked, I sadly yet shockingly responded, "His father was killed not too long ago." Dr. Simmons referred us to a Christian counselor. We scheduled a counseling session with Jeanette Edwards (shout out), a beautiful *and* saved woman who was anointed to help us through this dilemma.

During the first visit, she asked me to quietly sit in the room and she gave Andre' a few toy cars to play with and make him comfortable. She spoke to him about his dad and gently asked how he felt since his father's death.

Andre' proceeded to tell her that he missed his daddy. Her God-given gift of helping those who were grief-stricken was evident, and she softly asked, "Andre', have you ever wanted to kill yourself"? He replied, "No ma'am, not myself." She continued, "Not yourself, do you want to kill someone?" To my surprise, my son responded, "Yes ma'am, when I grow up, I am going to find the man who killed my daddy and I'm going to kill him!"

I could no longer restrain my silence and I cried uncontrollably. My precious five-year-old baby had murder on his mind and within his heart!

After the session was over, Counselor Edwards asked me, "Do you and your son attend church. I hesitantly responded, "We don't go *all* the time." She strongly recommended that I get Andre' into church... *for real*, not every other Sunday or on special occasions, but completely inundated in the things of God! However, Andre' [as a child] couldn't be introduced or sustain a relationship with God, without me being *his example*!

I wanted my son delivered from those murderous feelings. I didn't want him to grow up to fulfill one of the many negative statistics involuntarily assigned to black men or perceived to have "a chip on his shoulders." We as parents should desire to raise mentally and physically sound children that mature into whole and peaceful adults. Needless to say, I carried my happy hips to church and my babies went right along with me.

In the process of trying to make sure my children were spiritually intact, I too was delivered and surrendered my life to the Lord on February 12, 1996. It is imperative that single-parents are spiritually sound. We must be healed, so we *can* raise children who carry on their spiritual heritage to the next generation.

As Andre' grew older, he told me that he loved going to church and the things of God. I did everything I could to protect and nurture my children. As my children slept, I frequently prayed over them and blessed them. I spoke positively over them, anointed them with the oil, and prophesied God's will into their lives. I learned how to war against the enemy *for* my children!

Parents, we don't have to accept anything the devil attempts to plague our children with. I remember when my youngest son started having trouble in school academically. Deep in my heart, I knew he could do his work!

One day I began to pray and intercede on Donovan's behalf. The Lord revealed that there were some things spoken over my son to hinder his success... but God's word is sovereign, and it never returns to Him void!

Sometimes when we don't allow people to run our lives, they will speak cursed words against our lives. BUT WE must cast down every negative word and speak death to it.

It wasn't too long before Donovan's grades improved and he passed every subject satisfactorily. We serve a mighty God, and He has a master plan! I went to war in the heavenly realm for my son and his grades.

Intercession:

Dear Lord Jesus, I ask that you touch my brothers and sisters who are hurting from past relationships that didn't work or lost their spouse to an untimely death. You are able to heal the broken-hearted and cover their wounds with Your healing virtue. Heal them like only you can.

Give them a fresh start. Reassure them that you are the Royal Architect and you have constructed the plans to make their empty house a home, a temple fit for a King. Father, teach them to war in the spirit, so they can come against anything in their homes that is unlike You!

Help them to speak positive words of encouragement to their children and ultimately provide a very fruitful and spiritual inheritance. In Jesus name I pray. Amen!

Chapter 3:
Mama, Who's That Man...?
Introducing Jesus

Key Scripture: John 4:4-29(KJV)

Have you ever had a craving for something, but didn't know what it was you wanted? All too often, we go through life with a well of emptiness on the inside of us. Consequently, we try to fill these voids with unsatisfying substitutions. However, Jesus wants to meet us at the point of our need. He is the everlasting and living water that will quench and satisfy our needs.

I John 4:4-29, I believe the woman at the well, who is referred to in this passage, experienced the miracle of salvation! When she met Jesus, her whole life changed. She no longer needed the attention of men who were not her husband. Her self-esteem was renewed and Jesus introduced her to new worlds and took her places she never dreamed she *could* go!

When the Lord saved me, it became apparent to people who knew me that *something* was different. Going to the club six days a week was no longer necessary. Having meaningless sex was no longer a part of my life.

I began to season my words with grace. Oh yes, a change had come. To my surprise when Jesus transformed my character and my lifestyle, it caused others to be upset. When we no longer desire to do the things of this world, some people won't understand.

On February 12, 1996, I met the Lord. There were things I felt I could not accomplish on my own, but as I grew in the Lord, it was no longer a problem for me. Frivolous and casual dating were a thing of my past. Church attendance became my night out through the week. Instead of squandering my money, I became a financial sower, I desired to plant these seeds in the fertile grounds of God's Kingdom.

Most importantly, I brought my children home to raise them myself. You see, I had a set of twins in 1992 and their father had multiple infirmities. So, I decided it was best for our children to live with him during the week, and be with me on the weekends. Their father could not afford to pay child support. Furthermore, I was afraid of raising three children by myself. I believed the financial responsibility would be too much! I didn't want my children to experience a lifestyle of poverty, or a home reality that included inadequate nutrition, no shoes, no clothes or even a warm place to lay their head.

The decision to allow my children to live with their father in lieu of paying child support was a drastic mistake! Although, initially I believed it was for the best, I became the bad parent as if I didn't want my babies. However, now I understand, when notable changes take place in our lives, we're bound to make some enemies.

We must realize that the enemy (Satan) doesn't want us to change. Therefore, he will operate through people. These people will rise against us, and sometimes they are the people who matter most in our lives. Understand: asking Jesus to inhabit your heart, will cost you some relationships. Family members may get upset, friends may leave, but my dear friend, it's worth it. More importantly, your children will see and recognize the change.

My children started enjoying family time together and I believe the close bonds they established back then is the reason they are so close now. If I did not have faith in God (my provider) when I brought my babies home, they would have been raised in two different houses. The relationship between them would not have been solidified.

If you have children who are being raised by someone else, fight for your children. I believe that God sees us mercifully and when He gives us our precious babies, He intends for US to watch and care for them. There is something within you that God wanted imparted into your children.

If you are not in a position mentally to raise your children, get yourself together and bring your babies home. When your life has been out of balance for so long, sometimes it's hard to introduce structure. Structure consists of the things that God requires. As my eldest son Andre' says, "It was church twice on Sunday, Wednesday and Friday Night." Mid-week bible study and prayer became necessary tools to maintain our family structure.

If the children are younger, it makes it a little easier to transition into a kingdom lifestyle. However, when children are older... they may appreciate the change within their parent, but *may* not like or appreciate changes within the entire household because of their parent's newly-established relationship with Christ.

Curfews become bothersome, and rachet or thuggish habits are broken. The freedom to do anything and everything that child wishes, is not an option. Some children may think the godly-influenced structure is unfair, but it is imperative to help them understand that structure breaks generational curses, and releases God's favor to the entire family.

If you want to introduce Jesus into your family, you must first repent for not having Him there in the beginning. No, it's not easy to stay within the lines when a crayon is in your hand; but I guarantee if you keep trying and never give up, your life and your children's lives will become a work of art that God Himself will be proud of. Ask the Lord to lead and guide while you're rearing the precious blessing(s) He entrusted to *your* care. God won't let you down.

Intercession

Father in the name of Jesus, I pray for these single parents as they begin their life with you; raising children *can* be quite a challenge. Dear Lord please equip them with what they need to rear their children. Help them to grab hold of faith. The kind of faith that assures them they can do all things through Christ who strengthens them. Rain down financial blessings, favor, and miracles.

Break old habits and establish new godly habits. Prepare them spiritually, mentally, emotionally, and physically, for *this* task you've set before them. We believe you have all power in your hands and you're able to do exceedingly and abundantly above all that we *could* ask or think. We love you Lord and it's in Jesus' name we pray. Amen.

Chapter 4:
Mama, Are You Strong *Enough*...?
Depending on Jesus

Key Scripture: Genesis 12:1-3(KJV)

So, you've asked the Father for forgiveness and invited the Lord Jesus into your heart and your home, now what? In your early walk with Jesus, you will start to establish a relationship with Him. God will speak to you and you will recognize His eminent voice.

It is a beautiful thing when God's direction becomes your desire. You will yearn to please Him in every way you can. Your heart's desire will be to consistently talk with Him as your faith in Him is strengthened.

During my college days, I took a class and one of the requirements of this course was to be on time and be in attendance each session. On one particular day, I left my job late. I was about to get on the expressway and an approaching train (of ALL things) impeded my acceleration onto the highway ramp.

In my desperation, I exclaimed, "Jesus! I can't be late." Instantly, He reminded me... that there is power in the words I speak in Jesus' name. Before I knew it, I opened my mouth and faithfully declared, "In the name of Jesus, I command this train to be short!"

I opened my eyes, and looked up and the train was one box car long! I almost couldn't believe my eyes. That did wonders for my faith. With tear-filled eyes, I was reassured that I mattered to God!

As you continue your walk with the Lord, you will begin to go through what I call, "water-walking faith tests and trials." I will never forget the night I went to this particular church service, and God really spoke to my heart (I'd been saved for about two years). I could barely concentrate on the message.

As I sat in the service, He took me to Genesis 12:1-3. The words seemed to leap off the page. In that passage, God instructed Abraham to leave his county and go to another place that He had prepared for him and his family.

"My God..." I thought, "I know you're not beckoning me to leave my family? This is home! I have a good job. My children are settled in school... God, you *are* too loving to uproot me and my family from everything we've ever known?"

He answered, "Yes, I am telling you to do that. I want you to learn how to trust and depend on me. When you're in trouble or you need help, you call your family they come running to the rescue! I want to be *that* someone. The one you trust and depend on *with your life*. So, I need you to go to a place where you don't know anyone. There you will learn how to totally put your faith to work in me".

Two years prior, the Lord introduced me to a woman that became an intricate part of my life. My Pastor, my "Naomi," Apostle Dr. Cora B. Fells. I needed serious help and he knew He could trust her to give me that and so much more. But, living in Jacksonville and going to church in Palatka only one day a week on Sundays just wasn't enough to deal with my issues.

I talked to one of the sisters in my church and she and her husband agreed to allow me and my children to stay for the summer, so if I liked it, I could make my move. I tried reasoning with God and tried to talk Him out of it but, that didn't work – so I gave in.

I told the Lord I will move, but if Palatka didn't have a Walmart, I was going to move back home. I'm so glad our Lord has a sense of humor. I must tell you the year I moved to Palatka, not only did they have a Walmart, but the summer I came, they expanded to a supercenter!!!! God said, "Now there's no reason for you not to stay". What a mighty God we serve!!!!

The same year I moved to Palatka; my mother died. I believe she was my biggest fan. She would often come to my home and watch my children for me, wash our clothes, and cook dinner all while I worked. So quite naturally, I wanted her to move with me to Palatka. God had other plans but this reality still saddens me.

Learning to depend on Jesus alone was not easy. I didn't have my mother's help anymore. I became accustomed to paying my own bills... *on time*. I worked a full-time job, went to church, and prepared my children for school, church and bed! I cleaned my house and cooked home-made meals. Was this overwhelming initially? Yes, of course... but it was worth it! There is no greater feeling of accomplishment than being self-sufficient. God can do *this* for you too. Jesus' training camp has a way of making true soldiers out of everybody!

Right now, ask Jesus for forgiveness if you have depended on anything or anyone other than Him. The Bible states that He is a jealous God. Ask God to show you what changes He would like for you to make. He speaks often, but you must have an ear to hear.

Intercession:

Father in the name of Jesus, Lord I'm asking you to help my sister and brother solely depend on you. Give them the strength they need to wait upon you and study to know your voice.

Forgive us Lord in those times when it seems like we don't trust you and when we are not willing to make those daily sacrifices that please your heart. Teach us your ways oh Lord. In Jesus' name I pray. Amen.

Chapter 5:
Mama, *Can* You Jump Hurdles
Overcoming Obstacles

Key Scripture: 1 Corinthians 9:24-27 (KJV)

Have you ever been told, "Just give Jesus your life and everything will be alright"? Well, that statement is true... *in a sense.* You will have trials and tribulations, but the *"blessed assurance"* about walking with Jesus is that... He takes the burdensome weight *from* our heavy load.

It may be hard at first and seem like we're going crazy, because sometimes our backs are against a wall. It is during these times; we must walk by faith and not by sight!

Remember, faith can't see; it's blind. So, you must talk to God and tell Him all about your troubles. There will come a day when you retrospectively look back, and see that Jesus brought you through every situation that tempted you *to go back* to the life you once knew.

The year I moved to Palatka, my mother died, my maternal grandmother died, and my great-grandmother died. I was reported to "the state" twice!! I was fired from a job. I had to go to court... twice! To add injury to insult, I had to give the mechanic my car as a means of paying for the new transmission he put in it (go figure). I was evicted from my home and my daughter became deathly ill. Not to mention, all the while I was fighting a lust demon that I knew for sure had remained in Jacksonville. I suffered from depression, with and had to be delivered from anger and rebellion.

Every situation that came up in my life, Jesus saw me through it. Your story may not be like mine and then again, *maybe it is*. If you cast all of your cares upon the Lord, surely, He'll deliver you too.

My brothers and my sisters, anything worth having is worth fighting for. A wise woman (Apostle Fells) once told me that it's not good to want everything to be easy for you; because, as the common adage has proven, *"Easy come, easy go!"* Oh, but when you fight for your salvation and declare to God, the world, and the enemy that you're going to stand no matter what, *then* you know you have won the battle!

In Hebrews 12:1, it states: "Lay aside every weight and sin that does so easily beset you that will cause you not to be able to run this race with patience." Everything may not be a sin, but some things *can* be a weight. You have to be willing to go through for Jesus. Some things we bring upon ourselves. Not all of those trials I went through were the devil. There are things I caused myself and my children to go through. When we as parents don't know the Lord, we *will* make unwise decisions and our children are forced to suffer *with us*.

Intercession:

Lord Jesus, help my brothers and sisters to repent for allowing circumstances in their lives cause them to take a step back from you. Give them the boldness and courage to jump over every hurdle and obstacle that the enemy has strategically placed in their lives to cause them to fail. We trust you oh God, and we want to learn to lean and depend on you now more than ever. Continue dear Lord to teach us your ways. In Jesus' name I pray. Amen.

Chapter 6:
Mama, *You* Need A Man
Jesus, the Ultimate Husband

Key Scripture: Isaiah 54:1-17(KJV)

Out of everything I could possibly write about, I believe this chapter has to be my favorite. If you're not in that place to receive Jesus as your husband, this one's for you. It doesn't matter if you're male or female. The Bible says that we are all the Bride of Christ.

It is important to know the Lord Jesus as your husband, because in the world today, there is a substitute for everything; because we are impatient people. Sometimes Jesus takes *too long*, and we *are not* fans of the waiting game. We live in an "I see it, I want it, so I'm getting it, now" society. I want to encourage all of my brothers and sisters who desire the gift of marriage to ACCEPT NO SUBSTITUTIONS!!!

Substitutions will cause you to think they are helping, but in all reality, it's doing more harm than good. My friend, substitutions leave you empty and barren. They rob you of your self-esteem, dignity, self-worth and identity. The ultimate goal of a substitution is to cause you to never come into the knowledge of who you really are. Not who you are today, but the "you" that Jesus sees through His eyes of mercy and sovereignty. The enemy wants you to never obtain the promise that God has designed for you.

Always remember when a relationship is from the Lord, it will build you up, justify, and edify you. It gives you an "God-established" identity. It will cause someone to give you their last name.

In the year of 2000, I found myself accepting another substitute. Was it lust? Yes, it was... *the flesh is a mess*! A word to the wise, you can't dance over mess. The enemy sent him in a subtle way. I was witnessing to him and he said, "Can I have your number, so when I read the Bible, if there is something I don't understand, you can explain it to me." Wow, I fell for that!! When we're thirsty, we *will* fall for anything, because a substitute *is* better than nothing at all, right... Wrong!!!

Remember, what happens to you, happens to the children you're raising! If you allow someone temporary to come in your life, they are not a permanent fixture. Relationships that don't work are hard enough on the adult. How much damage do you think is being done to that child? Every Tom, Dick, Harry, Sally Sue, Mary, and Jane *should not* have access to your children! Children need stability and concrete interactions... so when they grow up, they will recognize and know how to maintain stable relationships *and not* jump from one bed to another.

In 2012, I had the privilege of visiting a remote area outside of Lima Peru. This was my very first mission trip, thanks to Anita Lenas and Laura Lebo, my two very special friends (shout out).

I was so excited that the Lord opened that door for me. When we arrived, I found out that most of the people were infested with pinworms. In Peru, homes could be built without paying taxes if the buyer agreed to leave the roof unfinished. However, *"the catch 22"* is... if you didn't pay taxes, you were not given indoor plumbing. Therefore, the water they consumed was contaminated with urine, feces, and only God knows what else! As long as the mission team was there, we could give them medicine, but our presence was temporary and the issue remained.

You see, in this case the indigent people chose to accept dirty water as a substitute, rather than paying the price for access to pure, clean, fresh water that would not make them sick! A little dirty water is better than having no water at all. After all, they were thirsty!

It is the same with us and Jesus. Yes, giving your life may cost you something, but in the long run, it's better for you and your children. Pay the price of committing your life to Jesus and wait on Him.

Allow Him to be the husband you so desperately want and need. Sell out your lives my sisters and brothers, because He already paid for it *anyway*. God wants to fill every void in your life so that one day you will be so full that you can begin to pour into someone else and help them to fully accept Jesus Christ.

After I repented for allowing yet another substitution to come into my life, the Lord instructed me to go on a fast. I did not watch television for two months; not even Christian programming. The Lord told me, *"You have polluted "your" land."* Therefore, I fasted for seven days and nights. He took me deeper in scripture and as I read, I realized several people struggled with harlotry (being whorish).

One day while I was praying, I heard the word "Betrothed" in my head. I looked it up and it means to be engaged to someone. Jesus began to tell me, "Try me, I love you. Will you please give me all of you, Let ME become your husband, and I will never leave you or forsake you." Jesus proposed to me!!

One day, as I prayed and studied the Word... The Lord led me to Isaiah 54. The words of the scripture spoke life *into* me. I finally realized that *I am* the Bride of Christ.

He changed my name that day and gave me a love like I've never known before. He did it for me and He will do it for you... *if* you let Him. Take the time to study God's Word and find out who you are.

In the Book of Joshua, you read about a prostitute name Rahab who didn't know the Master until the men of God came to her house and witnessed to her. She found a new identity and the Lord changed her life. He *can and will,* do it for you too!

Allow the Word of God to cleanse you, talk to Him daily and build a "real-ationship" with Him. Yes, I spelled *relationship* that way for a reason. Some people feel like they know the Lord, but they never get to know Him, *for real.* Don't play with it, because a real relationship with Jesus can make a *major* difference in your child's life.

My Testimony:

After my parents were divorced, we moved to another home and my mom went to work. People of God, divorce hurts everyone involved, especially the children. My mother found herself in the position of being a single parent.

This was a situation she wasn't familiar with. She was very depressed, over-worked, lonely, had financial issues which led to weight gain. This was a sure recipe for the enemy to attack her mind and her self-esteem.

Instead of her turning to Jesus, she found a man, he was definitely a substitute. In II Corinthians 11:14, it declares that the enemy can *present* himself *as* an angel of light. That's exactly what this *substitute of a man* did to my mother. When she brought him home everything was okay *at first*, but as we all know, the devil *can't* hide himself too long! He'd get drunk, refuse to work and then one day... the physical abuse started!

Yes, he started beating my mother. What mental capacity she had left, he eventually robbed her of that. She was unable to think or reason... and my mom became withdrawn. He had her right where he wanted her!

One night he told her he wanted me and my sister to start kissing him before we went to bed. As if that wasn't enough, he then told her he wanted to watch us bathe. His hands felt horrible on our bodies, and his lips burned because of the stinky smell of liquor on his breath!

No one knew the horror we went through in our home. I love the story of Samson when he was regaining his strength the enemy didn't realize it. All the while he was terrorizing our family, my brother grew older and became much stronger!

Needless to say, his reign came to an end when my brother took my NEW BATTON I'd gotten for Christmas and beat him over the head a couple of times. Yes!!! We were so excited because the police came and took him away, and that was the last we saw of him. I LOVVVEEE my big brother Alfred, and my sister Lisa. I can always depend on them to protect me. Alfred and Lisa, you two make my heart sing!

When we allow a substitute to enter the home, it not only affects the parent, but the children as well. DO NOT ACCEPT SUSTITUTIONS!!!

Intercession:

Jesus, my Jesus, give my brothers and sisters the heart, courage and will power to declare in their own life that they will not accept any more substitutions. Help them to understand they are the Bride of Christ, and you have a perfect plan for them and their children. Change their names oh God, and help them find an identity in you.

Lord help them to afflict their souls for a season, so that every yoke and stronghold of their mind can be destroyed. You did it for me and so many others and I know you will do it for them as you have no respect of person. In Jesus' name I pray. Amen.

Chapter 7:
Mama, We *Don't* Have Cable...
Learning to Sacrifice

Key Scripture: Ecclesiastes 11:1-6 (KJV)

"Girl, what are you doing with your money?" That is a common phrase often heard from my family. "I don't know" was always my response or "I'm just trying to make it." Once I gave Christ my life, He taught me how to prioritize by doing first things first.

I thought being a good parent meant buying your children a new outfit every weekend. I had a motto, "My children will not wear the same thing twice in 3-4 months." I felt that buying them things showed how much I loved them rather than paying rent and having a stable home life. I thank God, for delivering me from that warped philosophy! What does it profit a man to gain the whole world and lose his *only* soul? We must make sure we are not trying to overcompensate with "stuff" rather than giving our children love, discipline, and stability.

Isn't it amazing how low self-esteem can keep you broke? When our self-esteem is low, we *feel* like we have to dress up, keep our nails manicured, wear the latest fashions and hairdos, and drive fancy cars that we really can't afford – need I say more?

I had a saying that I lived by because I was advised by *an older woman* that it was "okay/normal" to use my looks/body to get the things I wanted from men. Due to her "guidance" my motto was: "Some mother's son will pay my bills, but my money is for me and my children to look nice." The men I "entertained," were viewed as my personal ATM machines. *Side Note: We must be careful of the advice we give to the younger generation. As mature older adults, we have the responsibility of planting good seeds in their minds, because they will do what we tell them to do, good or bad.*

True Testimony:

I had only one child at the time and my lights were off because I had to buy clothes, *remember?* Well, I called up two of my friends. One came earlier in the evening and the other, later that night. Both promised to bring the money back in the morning for my light bill. I didn't see them again for another two weeks, so my lights stayed off. Thank God my baby wasn't home (I never believed in allowing my children to see my dirt).

I can recall that night after they left, I went to the bathroom. I could barely look at myself in the mirror. My body was in pain from being used and abused all night long. I had been robbed of my dignity, self-respect, and my self-worth. I felt lower than dirt.

It takes the love of the Savior, Jesus Christ, to lift your head and give you back your self-respect after the world has stripped you of every ounce of pride you have left.

My family and my children's family were all great resources of help; but, Jesus wanted to be my main source of help. When God helps us… we don't have to lower our standards and sell ourselves short for a few dollars! We are able to wake up in the morning with a smile on our faces because the blessings of the Lord make us rich and adds no sorrow to our lives.

My brothers and sisters, if the Lord is trying to pull you out of your comfort zone and get you away from the way you've always done it in the past, let Him. He knows what He's doing. He can handle every financial battle you can ever face. Maybe your testimony is just like mine, or maybe you've tried stealing, selling drugs, lottery, and gambling; it doesn't matter. Try Jesus and become a tithe giver. Read Deuteronomy 14 and Malachi 3, it tells us what the Lord commands. Start sowing into the Kingdom of God, giving your tithe (10% of all your earnings), giving your offerings and watch God work on your behalf. When He blesses you, no man can curse you and you'll still have your self-respect in the morning.

It is important that we are not afraid of suffering. If we are going to reign with Jesus Christ, we must be *willing* to suffer. There was a period in my life where I was afraid of going without. I didn't want my children to have to suffer. Therefore, I made a decision to allow my twins to stay with their father because I felt that they would be taken care of better because everyone in the family had money. Suffer with your children. My Pastor would always encourage me by saying, "If you all have to eat grits and sausage together, bring your children home." I am so glad I listened.

As siblings, my children are closer. They wouldn't have the relationship they have now if they would have been raised in two different households. They know the value of a dollar. They learned from hardship. Children need to know that money *is made from trees*, but it *doesn't grow on trees!*

My eldest son, Andre' once said to me, "I love it when our lights or our water is off, or we don't have any groceries and then somebody comes by the house and brings us some food or turns the lights and water on.

Mama, I like seeing God work!" Oh, Sweet Jesus, that blessed my soul! There I was trying to protect them and they needed to see the mighty hand of God in action! We need to always instill good work ethic in our children; and *always* remind them, *"Easy come, easy go!"* Anything worth having, *is* worth fighting for.

Intercession:

My Dear Lord Jesus, I pray now for my brother or sister who finds themselves in a place of financial hardship. They probably don't know who to trust right now. Help them to find that place in you where they can rest in your everlasting arms.

I pray that you will lead them to a church home where they can be a part of a church family and begin to make a difference in the kingdom. Lord some may be fearful right now due to debt, but I declare and decree the blessings of Abraham over them and their children, all the way to the tenth generation. In Jesus' name I pray. Amen.

Chapter 8:
Mama, *Remember* ME...
Splitting the At/ten/tion

Key Scripture: 1 Corinthians 12:20-26 (KJV)

Have you ever heard the saying; *"the squeaky wheel gets the grease?"* Well, in the case of children, the one who needs you the most at that time, gets the attention. It is not that you love the others any less, but it is good to let them know that some things take precedence over others. This is common when there is a child who is sickly or has special needs and requires more of your time.

Every child has their *own* personality and *must* be treated as such. Just because one child may understand, don't make the mistake of assuming the other child does. Treat each child according to their personality. If he/she is a child who requires a thorough explanation, take the time to explain whatever it is to them.

The children we are raising now, are way beyond the old *"Because I said so"* era. Help them understand the reason why you tell them they can't have new clothes or shoes this week. Do not make the mistake of being condescending towards your child or anything pertaining to them. Their personalities *will* change *when* they feel unimportant!

Each family member is a different ingredient in the recipe of the family structure. Every personality adds its own flavor and texture to the household... and this concoction *must* be protected. In my profession, I have seen depressed children who desire the attention of their parents, but instead they are constantly pushed to the side.

Eventually, a spirit of sadness will cause their personality to change. A demonically influenced and oppressed child will wreak havoc on a family. Remember, spirits are transferrable. Soon, the whole house will be in disarray because everyone will be depressed and very unhappy.

If a parent is unhappy, does that affect the children? Of course. Ever since *that* child was in their mother's womb, he or she had the ability to sense and feel. Have you ever heard the saying, "*If you want to know if someone is a good person, bring them around an animal or a child...*"

Never allow the cares of this life to snuff out the joy of parenting from your soul. Times can get so hard that it will cause you not to appreciate your children *being* children.

Do not allow the enemy to cause you to live with a spirit of dread. That spirit is designed to cause your children to grow up too quickly; thus, causing you to miss intricate details of their childhood.

Don't rush it, take one day at a time. Make the most of the time you have with each child. Find out what's special about each of your children and build upon that. Spend copious amounts of time preparing them to be the men and women of God that He created them to be.

Mark 5:1-20, another key area that is crucial in rearing children is to make sure you watch for outside influences and demonic spirits. Demons are spiritual beings without a physical body. These spirits oppose everything Jesus stands for and the work He has done. They are very strong unclean spirits that desire to be rulers in heavenly places, not the heaven where God dwells but what is known as "the spiritual realm."

When Jesus walked the earth, the Apostles made certain to include in their writings that Jesus had power over demonic activity. He cast out demons from those who were bound and drained because of the enemy.

It is very important when we notice abnormal activity in our children, that we don't allow it to continue. If your child makes a drastic change in his or her life... pay attention. **The following list includes some of the things I prayed for regarding my children:** decline in academic performance, depression, a withdrawn spirit, always desiring to be alone, despondent, piercing the body, tattoos, extreme hairstyles, colors, seem to be more concerned and closer to their friends (so-called), homosexual or lesbian tendencies, girls dressings as boys, boys dressing as girls, cutting of the skin, very materialistic, loves money, greedy, gluttony, desires to watch pornography, listening to vulgar music, masturbation, touching oneself or others who may be younger, drinking, smoking, drug use, desires perverted sex, anal or oral, anger, sadness, emotionally unstable, contrary attitude, defiant, disrespectful, watch horror or violent movies or videogames.

If you read Mark 5:9, the demon told Jesus that his name was Legion, for they are many. When a demonic spirit invades your child's spirit, it causes that child to do abnormal things. We as parents must maintain a relationship with Jesus, so that we are ABLE to pray for our children and command evil spirits to leave our children!

Jesus said, we would do greater works than He did. If you are not joined to a ministry that operates in deliverance, I suggest that you find one! Just as witches and warlocks train their students to operate their craft in the spiritual realm, Jesus Christ also trains His people to cast those evil spirits out! Deliverance is real people of God, and it *should not* be taken lightly.

Please do not ignore these signs because your child's spirit man is balled up in a corner being tormented by these demons. We must torment Satan and his demons (Mark 5:6-8).

We must remember that we are a triune being, just as our Father God. We are made up of:

- **Spirit:** Inner man, the real you.
- **Soul:** Mind, will and your emotions.
- **Body:** Is your flesh; 'it' houses the Soul and Spirit.

If you or your child's spirit man is not under the control of Jesus Christ, then the flesh will control it. But if the spirit man is free, it can govern the soul and the body and cause you and your child to walk in freedom.

Ultimately, our jobs as parents are to make sure they fulfill their God-given purpose in this life. Maximize every moment, take the time to cultivate, nurture, and rear your children because the years fly by and before you know it, they will graduate from high school and go off to college or pursue their chosen career paths. The nest will be empty, so keep your eyes open and try not to blink, because *it* happens quicker than you think.

As pertaining to discipline, make sure you consult the Lord on what merit of punishment is feasible. There are times when we can talk to our children and help them to understand the error of their ways. Then, as the Bible says in Proverbs 22:15, that foolishness is bound in the heart of a child, but the rod of correction will drive it far from them. We *must* discipline our children if we love them.

The Bible says in Proverbs 13:24, He who spares the rod, hates his child, but he who loves his child will discipline him continually. Love them enough *to not* let them have their way, not out of frustration or anger, but out of love.

Intercession:

Dear Jesus, I pray for those parents today who live in frustration while raising their beautiful babies. Strengthen and encourage them Dear Lord to continue to seek your face so they won't feel like giving up in the process. God, help parents understand that "easier," is not always better... and that there is a blessing that comes out of the struggle.

Help us not to miss this time in our children's lives because we realize Lord, we won't get those years back. We decree and declare that the enemy will NOT cause the joy of parenting to escape their souls. We thank you Jesus and we will give you the glory forever. Amen.

Chapter 9:
Mama, *Aren't* You *Proud* of Me...
The Finished Product

Key Scripture: 1 Romans 8:28 & Philippians 1:6 (KJV)

As the saying goes, good things come to those who wait. While we've had our share of tragedy and heartache, tests and trials, we enjoyed some good times too. I am so proud of my children. All three have college degrees. I have gained a daughter-in-law, and I have some beautiful grandchildren who are dear to my heart. These are the years when you learn how to cut the apron strings and allow your children to live their own lives.

In the midst of helping my children be better, the Lord also brought destiny and purpose out of my life. I preached my trial sermon in 2006, and I married my dear husband, Bobby, in 2007.

It may seem like this era in your life is going to last forever, but enjoy the time you have been given to prepare them for the world. The ways of the world *can* be lethal to an *unprepared* child.

Use every situation that has come up to make you a better person. We *should* gain wisdom from our experiences. These lessons can help others overcome tragic situations.

Your life is a testimony *of how* God can take the things that the enemy meant for harm, and turn them around for *your* good. Only be thou strong and very courageous, always *keeping* God first, and you will make it through. I promise it gets better!

Intercession:

Lord, I pray that you consistently remind us that everything we go through whether good, bad, or indifferent... causes us to be stronger, wiser, and draw us closer to you and your purpose for our lives. Increase our faith in you and help us to always trust that you're working everything out for our good in Jesus name. Amen.

Chapter 10:
Mama, I Remember *When*...
Leaving a Legacy

Key Scripture: Joshua 24:14-15 (KJV)

The Bible says in Proverbs 13:22 that a good man leaves an inheritance for his children. I am sure we always attribute *this* to money; however, we as the righteous should also leave an inheritance of biblical principles as well, so that our children follow and ascertain in their walk of life. Remind them that when times get hard or storms arise in their lives, they can call on King Jesus to bring peace in those situations.

When my eldest son, Andre', graduated from college, he was already a husband, a father, and had a career. Life was about to start and it was not all fun and games anymore. He was now the priest of his home.

An unexpected situation occurred with his daughter, and I had to remind him that he could no longer play this game of life *without* Jesus being his head. It was time to get serious with the Lord and victoriously lead his family in Christ.

Everything that Andre' had been taught at home and church, he had to put it into action. He had to understand that once you start having children, you are not living for just you *anymore*. Everything that you do or don't do affects your blood line. As Joshua did, it was time to go to battle with the enemy, but my son had to be real with Jesus.

Do not live a defeated life in sin and expect God to reward you. If you are not saved, sanctified, and Holy Ghost filled, surrender your life now! Tithe your 10 percent, so that the Lord can rebuke the devourer on behalf of your family. Be faithful to Pastoral leadership and the ministry... and help in any way you can to push the gospel of Jesus Christ.

Abstain from the very appearance of evil. Do what's right in the eyesight of the Lord. Be faithful to your spouse and refrain from scandal. Be respectful.

I used to tell my children that there's nothing open after 2:00 AM but legs and liquor stores. *If* you are out late, don't let it be because *you are* doing something shameful. Remember, what you sow into your blood line, your children will reap. Generational curses are real, *but so are* generational blessings.

My grandfather told me once to work hard while you're young, so when you get older, you can relax and enjoy the fruits of your labor. Overcome the spirit of laziness and the mentality of *"wanting something for nothing!"* Providing for yourself and your family is very rewarding. Always keep God first and make time for family.

There is a nursery rhyme that I have come to appreciate through my years of being saved. The story of the <u>Three Little Pigs</u> has a very profound meaning. One day the Lord took me to Matthew 7:24-227 and taught me what to do, *when* you plan to build your life, don't forget to build on a solid foundation. Lest the enemy will come and destroy everything you've worked for.

This firm foundation is Jesus Christ, the solid rock! He is the anchor that keeps us stable. Jesus is the root of David that causes us to remain grounded and helps us to flourish as trees planted by living waters.

Intercession:

My Lord Jesus, I thank you for all of the families that this book will touch. Thank you for trusting me to accomplish such a task as this. I speak to the hearts of your people who have allowed the enemy to give them a calloused heart.

I speak to every stronghold of the mind that tries to keep your people in bondage. I proclaim liberty to those who are bound, healing to those who are sick, and bound up! I decree and declare freedom from oppression, suppression, and depression right now in Jesus' name.

They will live for you and raise children after your heart. Every generational curse is broken now! I come against the spirit of unforgiveness, stubbornness, pride, and hate. We will love and help each other as a family is supposed to do. Let your will be done in the lives of your people as all of the glory belongs to you.

We dispatch your angels of protection in and around our homes, our children when they are in school, lest they dash their foot against a stone. We lift your name on high above every situation and circumstance.

I speak financial blessings over your people now, and Lord, as they prosper in the natural, help them continue to prosper in the spiritual. We bless your name and give you the glory. In Jesus' name, Amen.

Chapter 11:
Mama, *Why* Am I Here...
God's Will, *Not* Mine

Key Scripture: Romans 8:28-39 (KJV)

I must tell you, within the fifteen years I've been writing this book, there was never an eleventh chapter. I had just finished typing the last page of the final chapter (or so I thought), and the following night I couldn't sleep. Psalms 127:2, states: "God gives His beloved sleep," so *when* He *doesn't* allow me to rest, it means a few things:

1. Either, I have had too much caffeine in my diet, or

2. There is unrepented sin in my life; I don't know about, and I can't sleep well with mess in my heart, or

3. He wants to talk, and conversations with my Jesus take precedence over everything!

That night, the Lord began to tell me to let the people know that His ways are higher than our ways, and His thoughts are higher than our thoughts. God is the creator of time; therefore, He will not be governed by time. It seems as though when certain unexpected situations come up in our life, we want to take matters into our own hands. But, because time does not belong to us, some things *will* take us by surprise. It takes a force more powerful than what our finite minds can ever comprehend. For we know in part and we see in part, but the Almighty God, the Lord Jesus Christ, holds time in His hands! God is sovereign.

The Lord has our lives all planned out when we come. In Jeremiah 1, it states, "Before the Lord formed you in your mother's womb, He knew you." God knew who your parents would be, in what manner you would arrive, and where you would live.

I am dancing around the subject of "purpose and mistakes" to help someone understand that it does not matter what our path *has* been... God knows, what it will be! Therefore, *when* unwanted or unplanned pregnancies occur... I do not believe abortion is justifiable. There I said the "A" word. Making the decision to NOT have an abortion is not very popular *(these days)*, I know.

However, if you trust in the Lord and lean not to your own understanding, but acknowledge Him in all your ways, He will direct your paths. The encounter might have been a one-night stand, rape or maybe you just don't feel you have the finances right now. But the child that is in your womb, or brothers, that child that female is carrying in her womb where you planted the seed, *deserves* a chance to live. I realize you probably don't understand right now, but just keep reading.

Some babies are born into wealthy families and some are across seas in the poorest regions of the globe. But I have news for you, *no one is a mistake*! We are fearfully and wonderfully made. Although, life may not be a bed of roses, don't make poorer decisions that *will* complicate your life, by doing something drastically regretful.

I never had an abortion... but I *considered* it, in my past. Like many of you today, I was afraid and I felt alone. It seemed as if my life was over. But God had a master plan.

True Testimony:

I was 16 years old and I felt like I had the world by the horns. School was going well and I had goals and dreams for my future. Then I became distracted *when* I *met* him. The more time we spent together, the less I thought about my school work.

Young lady or young man, please remain focused and **don't allow** people and things to deter you. I fell in love very quickly and within a short period of time, and when hormonal adolescents fall in love, sex is almost inevitable... and what should be sacredly preserved for marriage, is squandered away in a few moments of uncontrolled lust.

Side note: People of God always remember that your body is a temple and it's a beautiful thing to WAIT until you are married before having sex.

It was track season and practice had begun. I noticed when I would run the stadium stairs or lift weights, my stomach would hurt. I thought maybe I needed to use the restroom. This continued on for about a month.

One Saturday morning I heard the audible voice of the Lord. I had fallen asleep on the couch the night before, and I heard the most powerful words ever spoken to me. I had no other choice but to wake up. He spoke with so much authority, yet I could feel peace coming from Him and I knew it was the Almighty God.

He said, "Feel your stomach". I was asleep, but I remember responding, "hmmmm?" God spoke again saying, "Feel your stomach". My hand slowly began to travel down below my navel and to my surprise there was a hard knot no bigger than my fist at the lower part of my belly. I jumped up and ran to my room so I could look in the mirror. There it was, my baby bump.

I cried and pleaded with the Lord, "Please, God... NO. My family is gonna be so disappointed and I have plans! I can't have a child now, I'm *only* sixteen!"

Well, after weeks of anguish, my child's father and I talked it over and agreed that the timing was wrong. We were too young to be parents and this is not how we wanted to bring a child into this world. Therefore, we decided I would have an abortion. Little did I know, God had other plans.

After all, why would the creator of the Universe take out time to wake me up and tell me that I was pregnant. He allowed my mother to intervene. You can call it motherly instinct or perhaps He gave her the same dream, but she knew.

She came to my school and picked me up. She told me I had a doctor's appointment. She totally threw me off guard, I had no idea she was coming. When we arrived at the clinic, she informed them that I needed to take a pregnancy test. They handed me a questionnaire and the first was, if your test is positive, what are your plans for the unborn child? By this time, I didn't know what to feel.

I was mad because my mother knew and she was making me do this, but in a sense, I was relieved because I have never wanted to know what it felt like to abort a child. My answer on the paper was abort it. We waited for a few minutes and they called my mother to the back.

If you knew my mother, then you know she had a tendency for being rather loud (my Gail). I knew the tables had turned when all of a sudden, I heard the sound of ripping paper and her loud, distinct voice yelling, "She will have this one!" My mother was far from perfect but I will always love her for keeping me from making the biggest mistake of my life.

Five months later, I delivered a beautiful 6 lb. 13 oz. healthy baby boy who stole my heart. You are probably wondering why is she telling me all of her business? Because I don't want any of you to make decisions that you will have to live with for the rest of your lives. God has a plan for these babies and He will take all of your mishaps and give you a mind-blowing testimony.

My story doesn't end there. Little Andre' and I were doing fine. I had just finished school, landed a great job with benefits, had a car and an apartment with a baby who was 4 years old. Then, I met someone. We began to date and as usual, it got serious really fast. We had talked about getting married, but it was before I got pregnant.

Yep, here I go again – young, pregnant, and single. How could this happen twice? Oh, by the way, did I mention I was on birth control both times? Remember, the *only* sure birth control is abstinence. After I told him that I was pregnant, he said, "I don't think we are ready for that." He had just finished college and started a new job.

So, we talked and decided, I would have an abortion. I felt like I was walking through life with a head full of helium. I was so perplexed and distraught because I did not want to abort my baby, but I felt the timing was all wrong.

One day I went to work and my heart was so heavy. There was a lady I worked with was a Christian by the name of Mrs. Hazel Reed (shout out). I confided in her because I was about to burst carrying that burden around by myself. Hazel asked me what was I going to do. I told her that the baby's father and I decided I would have an abortion. She didn't say anything that day, but the next day, the Holy Ghost wouldn't let her keep silent.

The next morning, she asked could she take me somewhere during lunch. We began to ride and nothing could have prepared me for what she was about to show me. There was a church down the road from where I worked with a huge lawn. People were campaigning against abortion.

On the lawn, there were hundreds of white crosses in the ground representing the millions of babies who lost their lives to abortions every year. As we pulled up, Hazel said to me, "Stephanie, I can't let you do this, because if you do, they will have to put another cross down for your baby."

Needless to say, I wept, profusely. All of the heaviness I had been feeling was released through my tears as I decided, I'm keeping my baby. I called the baby's father when I got home and I informed him of my plans. He said as he hung up the phone, "Excuse me while I vomit". He was afraid too.

Sometimes it's not easy for a man to step up and be accountable. Our brothers need encouragement as well. Later that night, he called and said, "Well, you should be having twins because I'm next in line in my family." I thought to myself, "This man does not know what he's talking about!"

At my first doctor's appointment, the doctor said your measurements don't match your dates. Surprisingly, the sonogram revealed I was having twins! I was flabbergasted and my twin's father *was right*. I was scared, nervous, and excited *simultaneously*.

God protected me once again from making a big mistake. I would have given up two beautiful babies. I thank God for my angels, my mother (Gail) and Hazel for obeying the voice of the Lord and helping me bring forth my blessings.

Now that I have shared my life with my readers, I hope I've encouraged you all so you *won't* contemplate making such a desperate and foolish decision.

I have talked to young ladies who have had abortions. They have nightmares, suffer with depression, use drugs and alcohol as a means of numbing the pain... and attempting to silence the demons of regret. The enemy, Satan, will present you with a way out, but then torment you for a lifetime!

Jesus wants to remedy that. Yes, I was afraid, young, uncertain about the future, but when I look at my three children and how proud I am of them, my heart is so overjoyed at how Jesus stepped in and caused everything to work out for my good.

My children are such a blessing, not only to me but their families, friends and associates. They are active members in society and my life wouldn't be the same without Andre', Donovan, and Donielle.

I have a daughter-in-law, Sandreea, and three grandchildren, Amaya and Andre III, and one on the way. *Remember*, we go through trials sometimes *because* we fail to do things God's way. But even in the midst of our mishaps, He's still God... Trust me, there *can and will be* a silver lining to your story, "When God Is Their Father Too!"

Intercession:

Dear Lord, I pray for everyone who may be dealing with an unplanned pregnancy. I command the hosts of hell to be silent, in Jesus' name. I speak to their minds right now as they are making a decision about what to do.

Jesus, let them know that you're able to bring them out with a mighty hand. Holy Ghost, dispatch your angels in their homes or wherever they are to minister peace and comfort to them. Calm their fears and reassure my brothers and sisters that you have a master plan. We speak victory over every trial and situation right now in Jesus' name. Amen.

About the Author

Stephanie was born in Jacksonville, Florida in 1970. Her parents are Gail and Alfred Johnson. She is the third child of six children. She is married to Bobby McCaskill and the mother of three children; Andre, Donovan, and Donielle. Stephanie, also has three adorable grandchildren that she loves unconditionally; Amaya, Andre, and Amar'e.

When Stephanie was 16 years old, she became pregnant with her first child and delivered Andre in her senior year of high school. Because he was her first child, she didn't feel secure sending him to daycare so young. Therefore, she dropped out of school [temporarily], and one year later obtained her high school diploma.

She continued her educational pursuits, and took college courses to become a medical assistant. Stephanie, has worked in the medical field for more than three decades.

Stephanie, gave her life to Jesus Christ in 1996; under her pastor, Apostle Dr. Cora B. Fells and joined Grace and Truth Deliverance Ministries. In the summer of 1998, the Lord called her the move to Palatka, Florida. During this time, she lost her mother to a massive heart attack.

After years of serving on various auxiliaries within her church: the choir, the praise team, and the women's ministry... she delivered her trial sermon in the year 2000 and became a licensed minister in 2006.

Mrs. McCaskill, met her husband when she joined her church and they unified in holy matrimony in 2007. Stephanie, still ministers and evangelizes within the Putnam County prison system, the nursing home ministry, and as a personal motivator of single parents. Stephanie, is simply a loving and caring individual who helps others, from her heart!

www.ingramcontent.com/pod-product-compliance
Lightning Source LLC
Chambersburg PA
CBHW071316080526
44587CB00018B/3248